A plausible mission of artists is to make people appreciate being alive at least a little bit.
[When] asked if I know of any artists who pulled that off, I reply, "The Beatles did."

—writer Kurt Vonnegut

THE BEATLES WERE FAB
(AND THEY WERE FUNNY)

BY **KATHLEEN KRULL** & **PAUL BREWER**

ILLUSTRATED BY **STACY INNERST**

HARCOURT CHILDREN'S BOOKS
HOUGHTON MIFFLIN HARCOURT
BOSTON NEW YORK 2013

Music was everywhere in Liverpool, where

John Lennon,
Paul McCartney,
George Harrison,
and Ringo Starr

grew up. Life wasn't easy in that scruffy city in northern England in the 1940s and '50s, but music made things better. John played guitar and harmonica. Paul started out playing trumpet, but traded it for guitar. George had a guitar, too—and could play circles around John and Paul. Ringo was the best drummer in Liverpool.

From the time they got together as lads until they became superstars, the Fab Four made music, made history, and made people laugh.

PENNY LANE
18

John, Paul, George, and Ringo always had fun together, even when they were trying to name their band.

In 1960, they finally decided to call themselves the Beatles.

The name made them laugh—and it stuck.

In their early days, the Beatles performed for hours and hours in hundreds and hundreds of shows around England and Germany. It was exhausting and paid next to nothing. Anxious to have a record of their very own, the Beatles were afraid the band was going nowhere. They used silliness to help keep their spirits up. John would shout, "Where are we going, lads?"

"To the top, Johnny!"

"And where is that?"

"The toppermost of the poppermost!" the others would yell—and they went on with the show.

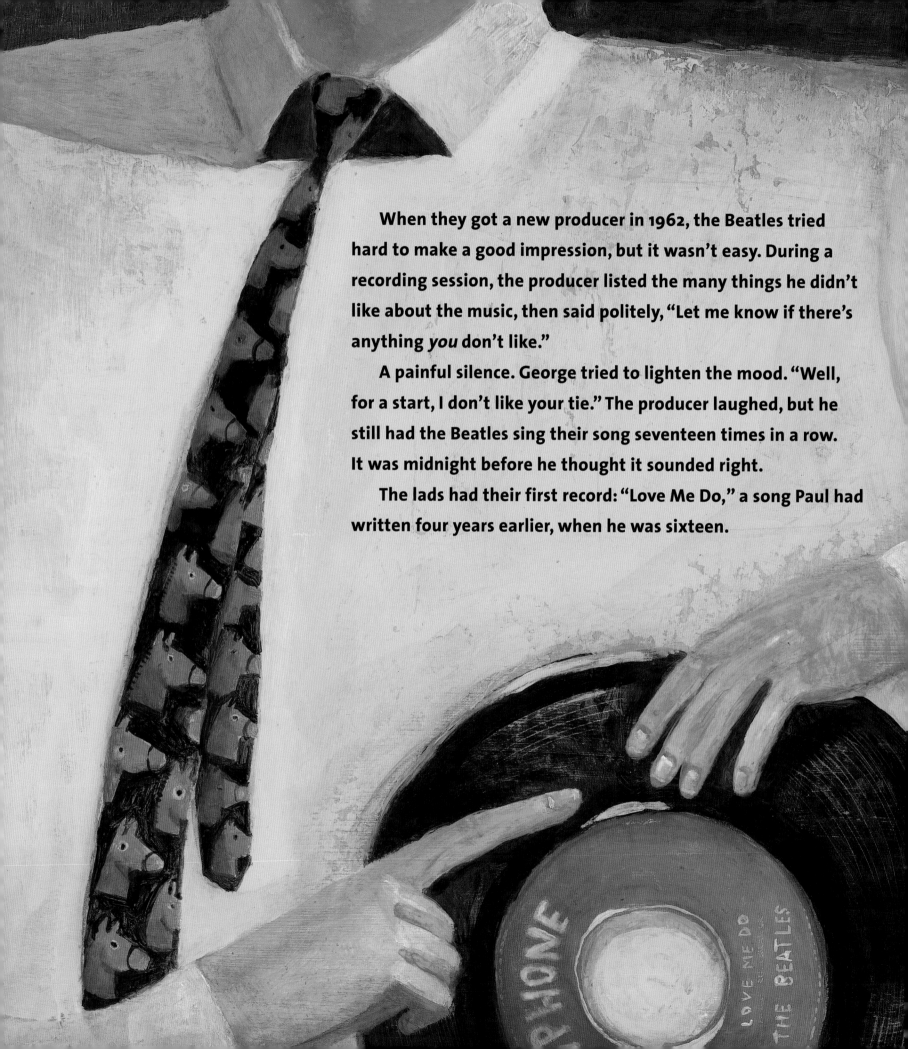

When they got a new producer in 1962, the Beatles tried hard to make a good impression, but it wasn't easy. During a recording session, the producer listed the many things he didn't like about the music, then said politely, "Let me know if there's anything *you* don't like."

A painful silence. George tried to lighten the mood. "Well, for a start, I don't like your tie." The producer laughed, but he still had the Beatles sing their song seventeen times in a row. It was midnight before he thought it sounded right.

The lads had their first record: "Love Me Do," a song Paul had written four years earlier, when he was sixteen.

Once the bouncy tune got on the radio, people started listening. Months later, the Beatles' second record, "Please Please Me," hit number one on the charts in England. The band began appearing on English TV, singing, joking, shaking their mop-top hair, and having a blast. The songs were fantastic, but the lads themselves were so cool, so funny, so fab—short for fabulous—that reporters started calling them the Fab Four.

The first Beatles fan club started with thirty-five members and grew to forty thousand within a year. Fans sent their heroes love letters, stuffed animals, and their favorite English candy—squishy jelly babies.

It was the birth of something new: Beatlemania. No one had seen or heard a band quite like the Beatles before. Fans followed them everywhere. The lads became clever at escaping crowds, although sometimes they needed help. Once a police officer slung Ringo over his shoulder to get him to safety.

The fans wanted more, so John and Paul wrote songs as fast as they could, meeting over tea and corn flakes. As certain words popped up in hit after hit, they began to consider them lucky: *me, please, love,* and especially *you.*

When they wrote "She Loves You," Paul's father begged them to change its *"yeah, yeah, yeah"* line to a more proper *"yes, yes, yes,"* but Paul laughed the idea off with a *"no, no, no."* "Yeah, yeah, yeah" was soon heard around the world, and "She Loves You" became the first Beatles record to sell a million copies.

The Beatles were no longer playing in small seedy clubs. They were even invited to perform for a formal audience that included the British royal family. How should they act? Could the Fab Four still be silly in front of royalty?

Before "Twist and Shout," their final song, John invited the main-floor audience to clap along. Then he peered up at the dignified royal family in the box seats. "And the rest of you, if you just rattle your jewelry."

Everyone giggled—even the Queen Mother.

Fame came upon them so quickly that the Beatles still couldn't believe it when they heard themselves on the radio. Whenever a Beatles song was scheduled to air, they would stop whatever they were doing, even driving, to listen to the radio with delight.

One night in 1964, their manager burst into their hotel rooms at three a.m., waving a telegram from New York in their sleepy faces. Their newest song, "I Want to Hold Your Hand," had hit number one in America. The lads stayed awake for hours, stunned that Beatlemania had crossed the Atlantic Ocean.

But John still had to joke. He liked to call the song "I Want to Hold Your Nose."

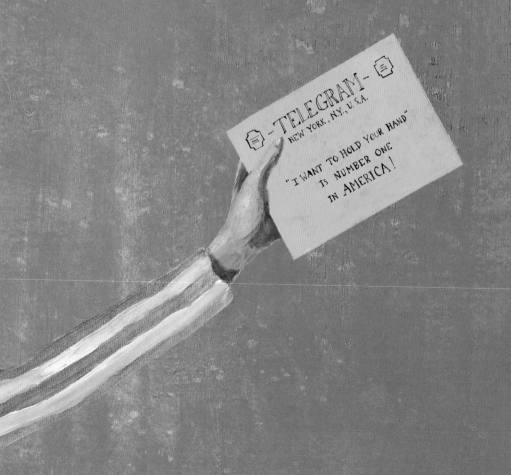

I want to Hold Your Hand
I want to HOLD your Hand
I WANT TO HOLD
YOUR HAND
Me, too
I want to Hold Your Hand
I want to hold your hand
I WANT TO HOLD YOUR HAND
I want to hold your hand
I want to Hold your Hand
I want to hold your hand
I want to hold your hand.

The next month the Fab Four flew to New York, arriving at John F. Kennedy Airport to the sound of three thousand fans singing, *"We love you, Beatles, oh, yes, we do!"* Two days after crossing the Atlantic, they made their first American TV appearance on *The Ed Sullivan Show*. By then the Beatles had played together more than a thousand times. Their performance was as polished as could be, and this turned out to be the most-watched TV show in history.

She Loves You

Till There Was You

I SAW Her Standing there

All my Loving

I Want to Hold YOUR HAND

Even when the massive audience in America made them nervous, the Beatles didn't show it. All the screaming of the fans was music to their ears—a sign that everyone was having a good time. George said, "We like screams, so scream louder and louder."

They were now big stars riding around together in limousines, yet the Beatles had as much silly fun as they'd had as boys in Liverpool.

Paul said, "There were just four of us in the back of that car, laughing hysterically." Laughter was their way of dealing with their sudden fame. They joked about everything, but they soon regretted joking about their favorite candy. Soft English jelly babies couldn't be bought in America, so fans started stocking up on jellybeans. They threw jellybeans at the stage during concerts as a way to show their love. Ouch! Jellybeans were much harder than squishy jelly babies. John had an idea: Just eat them.

The Beatlemania roller coaster reached dizzying heights during the 1964 tour. Fans screamed in the Hollywood Bowl, an outdoor stage under the stars; in Denver's Red Rocks Amphitheatre, the music echoing off cliffs of red and orange; in Philadelphia's Convention Hall, in a city filled with history; at the Indiana State Fair, amid the sound and smell of farm animals; and in nineteen more cities from San Francisco to New York.

Beatlemania was so intense that the screaming of the fans often drowned out the songs. The lads found it hilarious that the less their music could be heard, the more popular they became and the more money they were paid. Anything they touched went on sale to fans—even the hotel sheets they slept on were cut into tiny squares and sold as souvenirs.

Excited fans didn't just miss hearing the music. Sometimes people were so starstruck they didn't hear anything the Beatles said at all. John once tested this by telling a distracted restaurant waiter, "I'd like a steak, medium, and two elephants came and a policeman bit my head off, and a cup of tea, please."

Reporters interviewed the band constantly. The Fab Four often thought the questions were silly—and they loved to give silly answers.

Q: Which one are you?
John: Eric.

E very fan had a favorite Beatle.
John was often called the smart one.

Q: Some people think your haircuts are un-American.

John: Well, it was very observant of them, because we aren't American, actually.

Q: How do you find all this business of having screaming girls following you all over the place?
George: Well, we feel flattered...
John: ... and flattened.

Q: Do you go to the barber at all?
Paul: Just to keep it trimmed. But sometimes we do it ourselves, you know.
John: With our feet.

Baby-faced Paul was the cute Beatle.

Q: What is your favorite sport?
Paul: Sleeping.

Q: Is your hair real?
Paul: Is yours??

Q: You Beatles have conquered five continents. What do you want to do next?
Paul: Conquer six.

Q: Will you ever stop being Beatles?
Paul: We are the Beatles. That's what we are.

Younger and a bit shyer, George was sometimes the quiet Beatle.

Q: What do you call your hairstyle?

George: Arthur.

Q: What do you do when you're cooped up in a hotel room?

George: We ice-skate.

Q: If one of you stopped being a Beatle, what do you think you'd do?

George: I think I'd train elephants in the zoo.

Q: What do you do with all the money that you make?

George: I'm going to change all mine into cents, fill up a room, and dive in it.

Nothing rattled Ringo, even rude questions about his large nose.

Q: What do you think of Beethoven?
Ringo: Great. Especially his poems.

Q: How many of you are bald, that you have to wear those wigs?
Ringo: All of us.

Q: How did you find America?
Ringo: We went to Greenland and made a left turn.

The Beatles' 1965 American tour opened with the biggest live concert in history so far. A happy crowd of 55,600 fans welcomed them to Shea Stadium in New York. The band's helicopter landed nearby as they watched thousands of flashbulbs light up the sky.

This was surely the "toppermost!" And yet, with the wall of screams, nothing else could be heard—not the music, and not even the jets taking off from two nearby airports. This struck the Beatles as so ridiculous that they could do nothing but laugh. But they soon stopped joking, worried about the crowd getting out of control.

Later, a reporter asked, "Where would you like to go that you haven't gone yet?"

John said, "Home."

Four years after "Love Me Do," Beatlemania had driven fans wild all over the world. But the Fab Four were forgetting how to laugh. Concerts had bigger problems than jellybeans flying through the air. Now the lads were in danger of being trampled by excited fans.

At the same time, as they wrote songs that dug deeper into the meaning of life and love, their music was becoming too complicated to perform live. During their last major concert, at Candlestick Park in San Francisco, the fans huddled together on a chilly night. No one quite realized it, but Beatlemania was coming to an end.

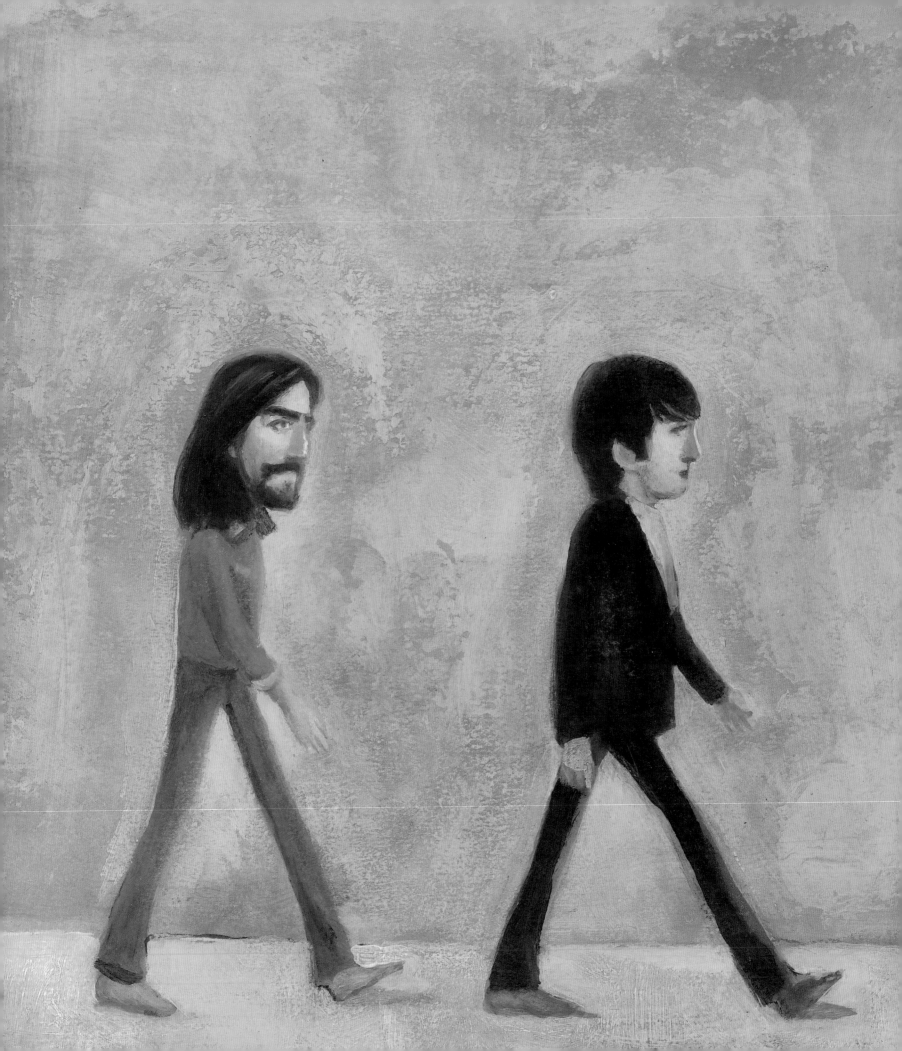

But it was far from the end of the Beatles and their fun-filled romp. The band retreated to the recording studio, where they could hear the music again and continue to make each other laugh.

Nothing was quite the same after Beatlemania. Other British bands became popular, but the witty wordplay of the Fab Four put them in a class of their own. They were trendsetters; everyone wanted haircuts like theirs, and everyone wanted to dress like they did. But most important, they're considered by many to be the greatest rock-and-roll band of all time. Constantly adapting their own music in an extraordinary display of styles and subjects, the Beatles changed music forever.

John, Paul, George, and Ringo

recorded more than two hundred songs together. For decades after, their music would inspire people to sing along, dance, love, remember, cry, think, imagine—and laugh.

IMPORTANT DATES IN BEATLES HISTORY

1940 Ringo Starr (Richard Starkey) born

1940 John Lennon born

1942 Paul McCartney born

1943 George Harrison born

1956 John Lennon forms the Quarry Men

1957 John meets Paul, who joins the band

1958 George joins the Quarry Men

1960 Band starts touring outside of Liverpool and changes its name to the Beatles

1962 First recording contract signed, Ringo joins the band, and "Love Me Do" recorded, followed by many more hits

1964 First American tour, first appearance on the *Ed Sullivan* TV show, and twelve songs on the chart of 100 best-selling songs in the U.S., including the top five

1966 Last public performance in San Francisco, California

1967 Release of their milestone album *Sgt. Pepper's Lonely Hearts Club Band*

1970 Last recording session, the Beatles break up, and the four go on to solo careers

1980 John Lennon is killed

2001 George Harrison dies of cancer

SOURCES

The Beatles, www.beatles.com.

The Beatles. *The Beatles Anthology*. San Francisco: Chronicle Books, 2000.

The Beatles Bible, www.beatlesbible.com.

Beatles News, www.beatlesnews.com.

Davies, Hunter. *The Beatles*. New York: Norton, 2010.

Harry, Bill. *The Ultimate Beatles Encyclopedia*. New York: Hyperion, 1992.

Kane, Larry. *Ticket to Ride: Inside the Beatles' 1964 & 1965 Tours that Changed the World*. Philadelphia: Running Press, 2003.

Norman, Philip. *Shout! The Beatles in Their Generation*. New York: Simon & Schuster, 2003.

Partridge, Elizabeth. *John Lennon: All I Want Is the Truth*. New York: Viking, 2005.

Sandercombe, W. Fraser. *The Beatles: Press Reports, 1961–1970*. Ontario, Canada: Collector's Guide Publishing Inc., 2007.

Spitz, Bob. *The Beatles: The Biography*. New York: Little, Brown, 2005.

Turner, Steve. *A Hard Day's Write: The Stories Behind Every Beatles Song*. New York: HarperCollins, 1999.

Womack, Kenneth, ed. *The Cambridge Companion to the Beatles*. New York: Cambridge University Press, 2009.

Text copyright © 2013 by Kathleen Krull and Paul Brewer
Illustrations copyright © 2013 by Stacy Innerst

Harcourt Children's Books is an imprint of Houghton Mifflin Harcourt Publishing Company.

www.hmhbooks.com

The text in this book was set in The Sans Extra Bold.
The illustrations were done in acrylic and ink.
The display type was set in Klickclack.

Library of Congress Cataloging-in-Publication Data
Krull, Kathleen.
The Beatles were fab (and they were funny) / by Kathleen Krull and Paul Brewer ; illustrated by Stacy Innerst.
p. cm.
ISBN 978-0-547-50991-4
1. Beatles—Juvenile humor. 2. Rock musicians—England—Juvenile humor. 3. McCartney, Paul—Juvenile humor. 4. Harrison, George, 1943–2001—Juvenile humor. 5. Starr, Ringo—Juvenile humor. 6. Lennon, John, 1940–1980—Juvenile humor. I. Brewer, Paul, 1950– II. Innerst, Stacy, ill. III. Title.
IV. Title: Beatles were fab.
ML3930.B39K78 2013
782.42166092'2—dc23
2012025483

Manufactured in China
SCP 10 9 8 7 6 5 4 3 2 1
4500391171

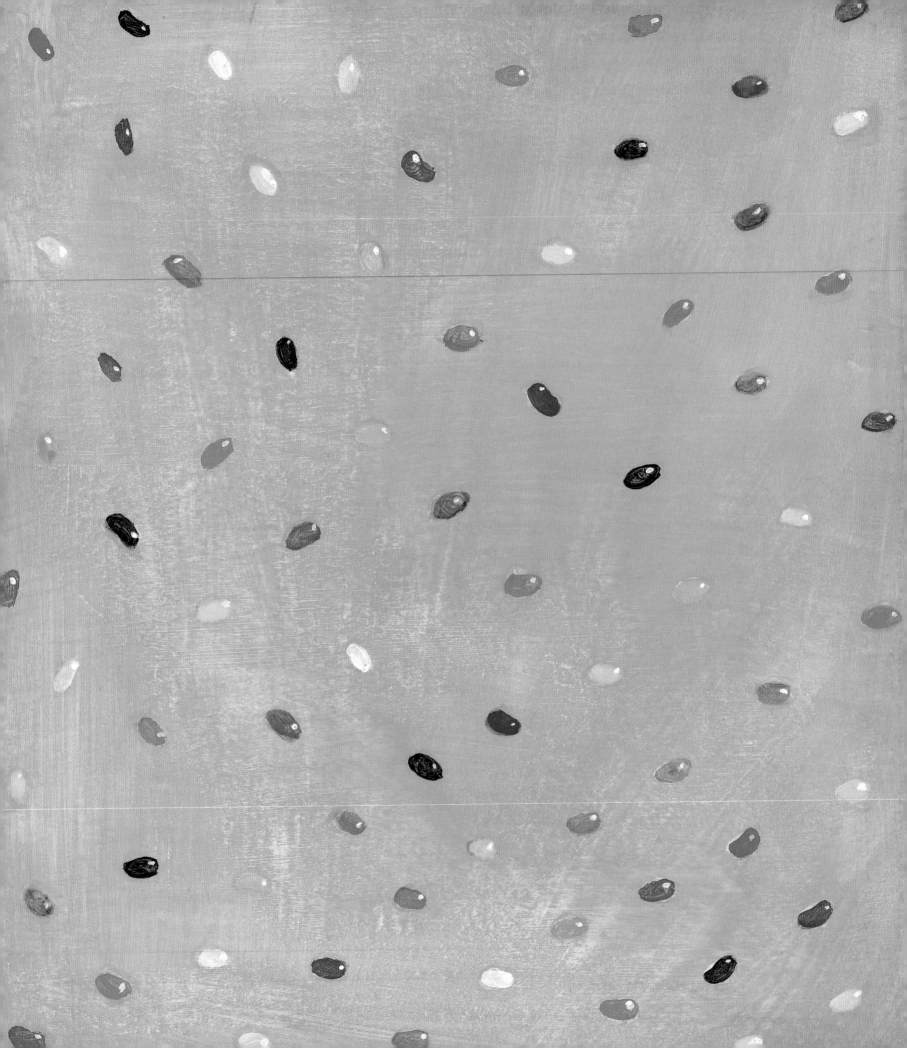